How to Start and Succeed as a

Silver

Entrepreneur

By Joe Schneider

Thank you for purchasing this book. There is a FREE gift waiting for you by going to: https://realliving.leadpages.co/gift-v1/

When you go there you will find a valuable download to support your success as a Silver Entrepreneur. At times the free gift will change so you may want to check back from time-to-time.

Table of Contents

Introduction: 7
    Inspiration 7

Chapter 1: Are You Ready to Become a Silver Entrepreneur? 9
    Should You Do It? 10
    Overcoming the Initial Problems........................11
    Success Is Just Around the Corner......................12

Chapter 2: The Advantages and Challenges of Being a Silver Entrepreneur 13
    Advantages..14
    Disadvantages 15
    Embrace the Advantages and Face Any Challenge 17

Chapter 3: What Type of Business Should You Start? 18
    What's Your Passion? 19
    Solve Problems....................................21
    Outside of the Box................................22
    Your Unique Opportunity 22
    Test Your Idea......................................23

Chapter 4: How Will You Finance Your Business?...25
    How Much Do You Need? 25
    Where to Get Financing 26
    Silver Entrepreneur Benefits 28

Chapter 5: How Do You Market and Sell in Today's Online World? **30**

You Need to Have a Strong Online Presence **30**

Website 31

Social Media 32

Blog **32**

Video **33**

Marketing Around the Push **34**

The Right Audience...**34**

Look for Competition **35**

Chapter 6: How Do You Stay Motivated? **38**

Look at the Progress You've Made **39**

Take a Break **39**

Exercise and Eating Right **40**

Think About the Future.......................................**41**

Never Give Up; Never Surrender... Why You Should Not Quit **42**

A Golden Opportunity Missed 42

The Horror, the Horror! 43

The Fab Five?...**44**

The Moral of These Stories...................................**44**

Chapter 7: How Do You Make Decisions & Solve Problems?..**46**

Good News for Silver Entrepreneurs **47**

How to Enhance Creative and Innovative Thinking **47**

Problem Solving System **50**

Step One: Define the Problem **50**

Step Two: Gather All the Information Available ..**53**

Step Three: Search for Ideas **55**

Step Four: Forget About It **57**

Step Five: Critical Judging 58
Step Six: Complete or Repeat............................59
Step Seven: Take Action Immediately 60

Conclusion 63

About The Author 64

"It always seems impossible until it's done."

-- Nelson Mandela

Introduction:

It's never too late to become an entrepreneur and start your own business. More and more seniors, over fifty years old, are starting to develop businesses after retirement as a means to fulfill their dreams or to make extra income. Just because you might be nearing your silver years, it doesn't mean that you have to think about retiring to Florida and going to early bird dinners. Even if your hair turns silver gray before or after entering your fifties you can profit from the lessons in this book. This could be a time for a new beginning, for creating the life you dreamed about, or to make a difference in the world.

Inspiration

Let's look at some names you might recognize - Ray Krock, Grandma Moses, Laura Ingalls Wilder, and Colonel Sanders. What do all of these people have in common? All of them were what we'd today call silver entrepreneurs.

Colonel Sanders, founder of Kentucky Fried Chicken, didn't start his finger licking chicken business until he was 65 years old. Laura Ingalls Wilder, writer of the *Little House on the Prairie* books didn't have her first novel published until she was 65. It went on to become one of the most famous and beloved book series of all time, and you are probably quite familiar with the television show that followed.

Grandma Moses, the folk artist, didn't start painting until she was in her 80s! The founder of McDonald's, Ray Krock, was in his 50s when he started what is inarguably the most famous fast food franchise in the world. Art Koff was 70 when he started RetiredBrains.com, a web site for seniors looking for jobs. Now in his 80s he still runs the successful business venture.

Each of these stories (and so many others out there like them) should serve as an inspiration to you. If you have the creativity and the drive, you can make it happen. In this guide, we'll be discussing the basics of what it takes to get started as a silver entrepreneur. You are never too old to succeed, and if the icons we talked about here are any indication, you can succeed BIG.

"The best time to plant a tree was 20 years ago. The second best time is now."

- Chinese proverb

Chapter 1:
Are You Ready to Become a Silver Entrepreneur?

So, you're retired, or perhaps you are thinking about retiring from your job. Maybe you've been downsized and are now out of a job through no decision of your own. No matter the reason, you no longer have your traditional job to go to every day. Some people might think it's time to sit back and relax... you've worked hard the majority of your life after all.

However, you aren't like most people. You want something more. You aren't the type of individual that can sit around and *not* be productive. Or you may want to give back to the world and make a difference. This means you probably have the makings of becoming a silver entrepreneur.

Retirement isn't what it used to be, especially from a financial perspective. You may realize that you need to have more money coming in to save and to help make ends meet. Getting a part time job isn't something that sounds appealing either.

Instead, you are the type of person that wants to take control of your life and start your own business. Being an entrepreneur is not merely a young person's game. In fact, you might find that you have some advantages, which we will discuss further in a later chapter. For now, we'll be focusing on whether or not becoming an entrepreneur is right for you.

Should You Do It?

Getting started is the hardest part. Many people have great ideas for a business, but they never follow through with the idea. They might think their idea isn't going to appeal to enough people, or that they are too old to become an entrepreneur, or they just don't know how to get started. Those doubts, (and the doubts of family and friends if you don't have a great support group around you) are what hold you back more than anything else, and they can derail you if you let them. So don't.

Take the chance, there is some amount of risk in anything you do in life, but do it smartly. You may already know what you want to do or you may still be discovering the best type of business for *you* to start. However, you don't want to go into any business venture without knowing what you are getting into first, which we'll discuss a bit in the next section and in more depth throughout the rest of the guide.

Overcoming the Initial Problems

When someone first gets the idea that he or she will start a new business, it's exciting and easy to stay motivated... at least for a while. Then the doubts set in, and they wonder if they are doing the right thing. Most of the time, this happens because they haven't fully thought through their business venture and they don't have a solid plan. They lose their motivation, and they don't employ enough creativity to help make their business idea unique. It falters and never comes to fruition. Even though you have a substantial amount of life and work experience, you still need to make sure you have a *business plan* in place if you want to succeed. The business plan I'm talking about here may not need to be a long formal document; that will depend on the type of business and the financial requirements.

You first have to define your idea and the type of business you want to start, and you need to be sure there is a need for that business or for the product that you are creating. Know your target audience. It will help with the direction, not to mention the marketing down the line. Even if it is just for a small niche, you will still have an audience and that means you have the potential to be successful.

As a part of your business plan, you should think about all of the other potential problems that you might face on your journey. How will you get financing for the business? Should you take a business class or read some books on running your business, or hire a business coach? How will you market and sell in today's online world? All of these elements are integral to your success. We'll be covering each of these, and more, later in the book.

Success Is Just Around the Corner

Failure is doing nothing. Failure is trying to get by on your retirement savings and Social Security while not having the money to do the things that you really love. Failure is *not* you. Inside, you have the drive to make your business soar. Success, for someone like you, is just around the corner if you are willing to take the steps to go and get it.

This guide is here to take you down the right path and to give you the guidance and motivation you need to get started, follow through, and succeed.

If you are working on something exciting that you really care about, you don't have to be pushed. The vision pulls you.

- Steve Jobs

Chapter 2:
The Advantages and Challenges of Being a Silver Entrepreneur

The number of Silver Entrepreneurs is growing. In fact, according to a report given by the Kaufman Foundation before the US Senate Special Committee on Aging and the Senate Committee on Small Business and Entrepreneurship, those aged 55 to 64 accounted for almost a quarter of the new businesses started. It's even at a higher rate than those started by people in their 20s and 30s. This has been true, by the way, in every single year from 1996 to 2013.

Possibly even more interesting in the same Kaufman Foundation report is that there are founders of technology companies in their fifties and sixties as well: one study found more tech founders over age 50 than under age 30.

This is promising news, and it certainly shows you that there is no age limit when it comes to a great business idea. Of course, there can also be challenges faced by seniors who start their own business. First, let's look at the advantages.

Advantages

One of the biggest advantages that silver entrepreneurs have, even if they are starting their first business, is experience. They've lived life, they know the vicissitudes of life, and this experience can prove to be invaluable. They bring a substantial amount of knowledge to the table.

Another advantage is that many seniors are more financially stable than their younger counterparts. More financial security can mean a willingness to take more risks when starting a business. Although it is not true that *all* seniors have a financial advantage, they may have had more experiences that make them better stewards of their assets.

Some seniors may have spent a substantial portion of their life in one job. While it might have provided them with a living, it may not have provided them with the ability to make money from something that they actually love doing. Many entrepreneurs today are finding ways to transfer the skills learned from past jobs or their hobbies and turn them into moneymaking opportunities.

Silver entrepreneurs also tend to have an established support system to help them. They have contacts and resources that they've been making for decades, and it is possible to utilize those resources to help get the startup off the ground. In addition, they have access to some resources that younger entrepreneurs will never have. The AARP is working with the Small Business Association to provide training, courses, and access to mentors specifically for seniors.

There is also the advantage of time. Many seniors are retired or semi-retired, and they have a substantial amount of free time on their hands. They could visit their friends, play golf, sit by the pool... or they could take advantage of their free time and start a successful business.

The excitement of a new challenge can be enticing at any age. Seniors tend to know their strengths and weaknesses as well, which makes it easier for them to know what they should pursue, and how to ask for help when they need it.

Disadvantages

Now it's time to touch on some of the challenges that silver entrepreneurs face when they are starting up their business. One of the big challenges they can face is "tech phobia". There is a misconception that seniors are unable to use the Internet, smartphones, tablets, and all of the other gadgets that people feel make the world go round.

While it might be true that some seniors have trouble with the Internet and other tech devices, it is certainly not the case with everyone. In fact, you probably have a good handle on the web, your phone, and your tablet. This "disadvantage" is quickly going away, and that's a good thing since you really will need to use the Internet to get nearly any business to become a success today.

Another potential disadvantage is that there does come some added stress and responsibility when you are starting your own business. For some seniors (actually, age doesn't really matter here), the stress can be too much to handle, while others have learned to cope with difficult situations better over time. A later chapter will provide a system for creative problem solving that will help alleviate this stress.

Health is another possible disadvantage for some seniors, but again things are changing today as we are living longer, healthier and more active lives than ever before. Even when Americans retire at age 65, they can expect to live healthily for another two or three decades.

Embrace the Advantages and Face Any Challenge

Largely, you have far more advantages when it comes to being a silver entrepreneur than disadvantages, and this should certainly be encouraging to you. You have what it takes to become successful if you are committed to working hard and developing a good business idea that you follow.

Does this mean that every silver entrepreneur will be successful? Of course not. Not all businesses succeed. Yours could though. Remember what Wayne Gretzky said. "You miss 100% of the shots you don't take." It is time you gave it a shot.

You may never know what results come from your action.
But if you do nothing, there will be no result.

- Gandhi

Chapter 3:
What Type of Business Should You Start?

Choose a job you love and you will never have to work
a day in your life.

— Confucius

Now that you are on board with the idea of starting a business, we can get into the fun part. What type of business should you create? Here's the exciting news. You can do just about anything your heart desires, as long as you believe there is a market for it. Even a small product or service geared toward a small niche market has the chance to succeed if you do it right.

You have a substantial number of options. You could buy a company that already exists and has an owner that wants to exit. You could buy a franchise or get into multilevel marketing. Of course, you might also want to start a new venture that's created entirely by you, giving you greater flexibility and independence.

It is not a good idea to start a business with just the purpose of making money. You may have some success with that type of venture but will lose interest in it before long. The most successful businesses have a strong commitment to making a difference, providing great quality and customer support. Having a guiding reason for providing your product or service will eventually come through to your customers.

What's Your Passion?

One of the best ways to find a business idea is to look at your passions and the things that you love. What are your hobbies? What do you do in your spare time? When you are able to turn a hobby into a moneymaking opportunity, you will find that you actually love what you are doing. This means you will put far more effort into making sure it is a success.

Make a list of the things that you enjoy, or that you have enjoyed in the past and had to give up for some reason, such as not having enough time. Add to the list the topics you would likely be reading about if you were stuck in a library with only nonfiction books and periodicals for a week. Your list can have anything on it that you like - do some brainstorming. Here's a sample list to get you started..

- Writing
- Film / video

- Pets
- Painting
- Comic books
- Electronics
- Golf
- Decorating
- Coaching
- Gardening
- Cooking
- Teaching

This is just a short list. Let's look at some of the ways that you could turn one of these passions into a business. If you like cooking, for example, you could start a business where you teach other people how to cook. Maybe you will teach young single people how to make delicious meals for one. Maybe you will create a YouTube channel and have your own cooking show that features your dishes along with your unique perspective, style, and sense of humor. Maybe you will write a cookbook. You could even become a caterer or start a food truck. These are just some of the possible ideas.

Another option is to take a skill that you developed over time in a previous job and teach it online or as a coach. It may be a way of organizing tools or data that could be taught online or in eBooks. You have acquired knowledge and skills that other people would like to have and there are many ways to monetize those assets.

As you can see, you can take your skills, hobbies or passions and find ways to turn them into moneymakers. Let your imagination go when you come up with your list of interests and possible business ideas.

Solve Problems

You have a lot of life experience, and in that time, you've probably come across quite a few problems with the way that different things work. Make a list of the common, everyday problems that you see around you no matter how small they might seem. You can bet that they bother other people as well.

Instead of just complaining about these issues, start to think about ways that you could fix them or make them better. Solving a problem could be a good way to come up with a product or service that the world doesn't even know it needs yet. Find something frustrating and find a way to remove that frustration.

Look at the story of Bookrenter.com as an example. The founder of the company realized that college textbooks were simply too expensive to buy, even used. So, he started his company that rents textbooks. The solution doesn't need to be complex. It just needs to improve the status quo.

Outside of the Box

While not all business ideas will work, there is no such thing as a stupid idea. Write down every idea that you have and then see if you can develop it. Some will fall by the wayside quickly, but others will bear fruit. Take each of the ideas through as many steps of development as you can to see whether they are worth pursuing or not.

Look for different niche categories where you might be able to start a business. Look at the things large companies are doing and find the customer base that they are ignoring. Then, market a product to that niche.

Your Unique Opportunity

A good opportunity for silver entrepreneurs to consider is digital information products. You have a unique set of experiences, skills and interests that is different from anyone else. There are always other people that would like to have some of the information that you know and are willing to pay for it. One of the fastest and least expensive ways to start a business is by turning your experience, passions or hobbies into a digital product such as an eBook, audio program or video and selling it online.

There are several techniques you should learn to build a successful business in this market. There are many sources for getting the training and support you will need, including how to outsource the parts of the business you do not want to do yourself. If you are not a good writer there are people that you can hire at reasonable fees to write, or present your information in a video, or organize a marketing campaign.

Test Your Idea

Questions you should ask yourself and contemplate before starting your business:

1. What problem are we solving?
2. Who are our customers?
3. How important is it to them, its perceived value? Will they pay for it?
4. How good are we at solving it, and can we prove our/its value?
5. How easily are we replaced (the competition)?
6. What is our USP (Unique Sales Proposition)?
7. How easily can we identify and reach the potential clients?
8. And how will you close/convert them?

You don't have to have all the answers when you start. But before making a major investment of money or time you should test your new venture.

"If you just work on stuff that you like and you're passionate about, you don't have to have a master plan with how things will play out."

- Mark Zuckerberg, founder of Facebook.

Chapter 4:
How Will You Finance Your Business?

So, you have a wonderful business idea, and you are ready to get started, but… wait, how are you supposed to pay for all this? Financing is one of the most common questions and problems that entrepreneurs, silver or not, face when they are building a new business. Fortunately, quite a few options can help you find financing that can get your business off the ground.

Let's look at some of the different ways that you can finance your business, and whether you need to have much financing in the first place.

How Much Do You Need?

How much money will you need when you start your business? It's important to be as accurate as possible when you are trying to assess the amount of money you will need for the startup, even though this can be difficult. It generally depends on the type of business you are starting and what you already have in place in terms of equipment and supplies.

If you wanted to go into writing for the web, you wouldn't need much more than a computer and an Internet connection, which you already likely have. You wouldn't need to borrow or dip into savings to do this.

However, if you wanted to buy a franchise, you would need a minimum of $10,000, and likely much more.

Know how much you need, and then start looking for the financing you need.

Where to Get Financing

You can find financing from a number of sources. You could dip into your retirement savings, ask for a personal loan from a friend or family member, or even go through a conventional lender for a loan. Look for investors who believe in your idea and who are willing to put their money behind you. Some businesses may even qualify for grants either the government or foundations that are supporting a business niche.

There are also government organizations setup to help small businesses get funding such as the Small Business Development Corporation (SBDC). The US Small Business Administration (SBA.gov) offers programs to help seniors starting new businesses. And non-profits such as AARP.org and

Encore.org where you can learn about programs and opportunities designed to help seniors pursue business opportunities after retirement.

Another organization that provides guidance for entrepreneurs including business plan review and all aspects of business development including funding sources is SCORE.org. This non-profit was originally called Service Corps of Retired Executives but now just goes by SCORE; providing free business mentoring services to entrepreneurs in the United States.

Formal sources of funding such as banks and venture capital will require detailed business plans and to get a grant you will need to make a formal grant proposal. However many small businesses only need a basic, simple business plan which can be on a single page or two. Don't overlook the business plan because it will help you evaluate the business potential and requirements for success.

Here's another new option that you might want to consider - crowd funding. Through websites such as Indiegogo.com, Kickstarter.com, and dozens of others, you can pitch your idea to the Internet at large. If they like the idea, they can back your business by purchasing, investing, or donating money.

Other benefits of crowd funding are the ability to presell the product and test the market. Your crowd will also provide feedback on features that make it more or less appealing to these early adopters and help refine the product.

It has some similarity to looking for venture capital, albeit with a different scale. Instead of a small number of investors with large investments, there tends to be a larger number of investors offering smaller amounts of money. Crowd funding, like any type of fundraising, takes a significant amount of planning and preparation before, during and after the funding campaign. While it might not work for all businesses, it is certainly worth considering, so make sure you look into these sites.

Silver Entrepreneur Benefits

As previously mentioned, you have many experiences that come with many years of living. There are ways to turn those skills and knowledge into business opportunities that require little monetary investment. In addition to those already mentioned you could put your knowledge into digital products including: books, eBooks, online webinars, teleseminars, membership sites, or online courses. These products can be started with little investment and continue to bring income for many years with no additional time or effort – the "earn while you sleep" approach.

You may also share your experiences through speeches, coaching (either private or groups), or businesses training. Although you won't be paid if you're sleeping, they may require little to no investment with significant income potential.

One of the first things an investor looks at in a business plan is the management team. Your management experience, stability and success stories will be very helpful. You may also have friends, past associates or contacts in the industry that would join your team or be advisors or board members.

"Chase the vision, not the money; the money will end up following you."

--Tony Hsieh, CEO of Zappos

Chapter 5:
How Do You Market and Sell in Today's Online World?

Even when you have a great idea or product and you know that you can finance your business, you have to think about everything that comes next. Namely, you need to think about how you will be able to market and sell in today's world. Proper marketing will help you to increase brand awareness about your business. You simply have to make sure you are doing it the right way.

Keep in mind that your brand is about more than just your logo. It's about the overall way you want people to perceive your business, and it should be a part of your overarching marketing plan.

You Need to Have a Strong Online Presence

There is no doubt that the Internet is easily the most important element for any company, large or small, when it comes to marketing, and there is simply no getting around it. Let's look at some of the most important components you need.

- Website

- Social Media
- Blog
- Videos
- Email

Website

You can't get by today without a website, landing page or similar platform. Fortunately, it is relatively easy to get a website up and running since there are so many options out there that have templates to get you started quickly. You could also have someone else make the website for you if you don't have the skills or the time.

If you buy a franchise or join a multilevel marketing business you will probably have a website that simply needs your specific information uploaded. You may also have landing pages, which are sights on the Internet that are linked to a promotional ad, or your business card where customers can get more information or buy your product.

Your website needs to be full of quality content that features keywords and phrases that are associated with your product or business. You can search with the Google AdWords keyword planner to know what words and phrases will be the best option for your site, blog, and other online content. Then, just add those words and phrases to the content where they make sense.

Social Media

In addition, you need to have social media accounts such as Facebook, Twitter, YouTube, or several other platforms. The type of business will determine where you need to be and the time you need to spend on the account. Social media platforms are a great way to help you build your brand and spread the word about your business. It's important that you have separate accounts for your business and personal use though. In addition, once you start to get followers and fans, it's always a good idea to make sure you actually interact with them. It's a two-way conversation, or at least it should be if you want to make the most use of it.

Blog

Sometimes it will be useful to have a blog that is connected right to your site. A blog is simply a web log, a place where you can write posts about your business. The posts can be about anything that you like, but it's really best to keep them somehow related to your field. They shouldn't all be marketing related, as we'll discuss later. However, they should all be something that your niche audience will find interesting.

For example, if we go back to our earlier example of turning your cooking into a business, you could post a recipe a week on the site, or some photos of dishes you've made. You can even add video links from sites such as YouTube to embed the videos of you making the dish.

Video

Video might not be essential quite yet, but the world is moving in that direction, and it will be valuable for many types of businesses. YouTube is one of the most visited websites in the world, and having a channel and some videos on the site can help to increase brand awareness. You can even monetize the channel and make money from the ads it runs.

The videos you create, if you decide to go that route, can be about anything you like, as long as it somehow pertains to your business. You could do some fun commercials, start a show, create some how-to videos, and more. When you are making your videos, make sure you align everything with your brand.

Videos are also a great way for silver entrepreneurs to present expert information and training to customers. Your videos could be sold as webcasts or as a full series of video training course. Your content is more important than the video quality or artistic visual effects, unless of course your business is creating high quality videos. In many cases you can use the HD camera on your smart phone or a basic camcorder if you get a clear image and sound quality.

Marketing Around the Push

One of the most important things to take away from marketing in today's world, especially online, is that you can't constantly try to push your products or services. People do not have the time or patience for this, and they will let you know, or they will stop following you and visiting your site.

This simply means that you need to have interesting and useful content mixed in with your traditional marketing. A simple rule is that the actual marketing of the material should not account for more than about 20% of your online activities across all platforms. You want to give people useful information so they get to know and trust you. Then, they will want to learn more about what you have to offer.

The Right Audience

The most important thing to consider when you are developing your marketing plan is your audience. Who are you trying to reach? Who is the ideal customer for your product or service? By keeping your niche audience in mind and thinking about the things that they need and want, it makes creating a workable marketing plan much easier. It's even easier to come up with the right keywords.

While you might want your product to sell to everyone, it probably won't. Find your audience, whoever they might be, and target them like a laser.

Look for Competition

Competition can be good, necessary, or even provide a path to greater success. Depending on your business, you may want to find a niche market that has lots of competitors.

If you are creating a product such as a book, eBook, or expert training program you want to be sure there are other products selling to that target audience. Finding a small segment of a large market with many buyers and sellers can have advantages. You know there is potential for products with variations that differentiate them. For example, if you search "cookbook" on Amazon, there are over 183,000 books listed. And there are many more added every day. But there are also thousands sold every day. Do you know any one interested in cooking that has only one cookbook? There are probably 40 in my house.

Cooking, in addition to being a hobby for some, is also somewhat important for everyone who eats, so it is a very big market. Most hobbies also have many books and sources of information. Amazon has over 360,000 photography books, 3,600 model train books, and over 27,000 books on how to write books. All you need is a different twist, a unique solution, or to introduce a new concept and you can have a profitable sub-niche...as long as you have a good product and marketing strategy.

While some businesses, like a hair salon, may not want too many competitors on the same block, have you noticed how many car sales lots are found on the same street? They go where buyers are likely to see them and browse.

Many successful businesses have discovered ways to work with their competitors to benefit each party. Sometimes as affiliates, selling each others similar but slightly different products, joint advertising, or dozens of other ways to partner and profit from a potential competitor.

Going into a business where there doesn't seem to be any competition can be the riskiest. Unless you are taking established, well known products into a new geographic area, you may have the expense of getting the attention and educating the consumer on why they need your product or service.

Always learn who your competition is but also consider how you may benefit from the competition. Remember that the biggest competitor is usually the consumer continuing to do what they are doing without buying anything.

You have set yourself a difficult task, but you will succeed if you persevere.

— Helen Keller

Chapter 6:
How Do You Stay Motivated?

We've all had spurts of "fleeting motivation". You get a great idea that excites you, that you feel could be the next big thing. You get to work and then other parts of life suddenly distract you. The next thing you know, that motivation and excitement have dried up and vanished. The motivation to continue is gone, and you don't know it if will ever come back.

What happened? Motivation can vanish for a number of reasons, and sometimes it is actually wise to listen to them. Maybe you discovered that your idea wasn't as original as you thought or that the business wouldn't work for some reason. It's a good idea to take a step back and to reassess things. Keep in mind that we used the word reassess and not quit. Look at new ways of resurrecting the idea and turning it into a fruitful business or a successful product. A little tweaking to your ideas and your business plan can go a long way.

"Failure is just a chance to start again but this time more intelligently."

— Henry Ford

Here are some tips on staying motivated.

Look at the Progress You've Made

Maybe you haven't reached the level of success that you wanted at this point. Well, stop and look at how far you've come. You started with an idea, brought it to fruition, and you are actually following your dreams. When you take some time every once in a while to appreciate the progress you've made, it helps you to put things into perspective. You might not be as far along on your journey as you hoped, but you *are* getting somewhere. This should help to spur you on further.

Something that you might want to do is come up with some "mini-milestones". These goals are the smaller and more frequent milestones that you can latch onto like rungs on a ladder to pull you upward. They can make you feel as though you are moving forward at an even faster pace.

Take a Break

Sometimes, you have to know when to step away from the work and take a break. One of the potential problems of being an entrepreneur is that you are always thinking about work. You need to have some time where you can simply unwind and relax. A good option for this is to learn to meditate and make it part of your daily routine.

It doesn't have to be meditation. It could simply be sitting outside with a cup of tea and thinking about anything except your work. Maybe it's talking with some friends or family. The point is to make sure that you are taking some time for yourself. You will find that this helps to recharge your batteries so you can move forward with your project with renewed vigor.

Exercise and Eating Right

Staying physically active helps to increase your energy levels, and it helps to relieve stress. When you do this, you will find that it naturally helps to increase your levels of motivation. Exercise is another way to develop, and it ensures you are staying healthy so you can take your business to the top.

The type of exercise you choose can vary widely, but it's always a good idea to talk with a doctor before you start any type of exercise program. Some options that you might want to think about as part of your exercise regimen include swimming, walking and hiking, classes at the gym, golf, weight lifting, and biking. Just find something, or multiple activities, that you enjoy and make time for them each day if you can. If you find that you have a very busy schedule, you should at least try to get in an hour a day, three or four days a week.

You should also consider your diet. Eating healthy makes you feel better, and you will find when you combine it with exercise, it not only changes your body, but also your mind. Together, diet and exercise really can help to boost your motivation levels.

Think About the Future

Some people live in the past and they continue to reflect on their failures. This does nothing but stall their growth. Others live entirely in the here and now, and while that does mean that they are able to experience and enjoy life as it comes at them, it's not a good idea to think only about the present. The present is for the work you are doing now. Thinking about the future, and envisioning a positive future can help you to forge your path toward actually making it a reality.

It's about knowing your goals and visualizing them coming true through your hard work. It is surprising just how motivating this can really be.

Never Give Up; Never Surrender... Why You Should Not Quit

Here is something you should always keep in the back of your mind. *It is always too soon to quit.* You never know what tomorrow could bring. Tomorrow could be the day you get the big break that you and your business need. Or maybe it won't come until the day after tomorrow. The point is that you will never know when your success will arrive if you quit now.

Let's look at a couple of stories that help to illustrate this point. Something that's important to remember is that you don't hear many stories about people quitting too soon *because they never realize the opportunities they missed*. They vanish into the ether. You don't want to be someone who wonders what could have been, and that alone should be reason to stick with your new business.

A Golden Opportunity Missed

First, we'll paraphrase a story that was featured in a book called *Think and Grow Rich* by Napoleon Hill. It's about a man who headed West during the gold rush, hoping to strike it rich. He found a bit of gold and was thrilled. He and others continued to dig but couldn't find the vein of gold, where the real riches waited for them. Instead of persevering, he gave up. He sold his equipment, packed up and went home. The man to whom he sold the equipment had a mining engineer look at the mine. The engineer said the others failed because they didn't understand fault lines. It turned out there were a mere three feet away from gold. This turned out to be one of the world's richest gold minds.

This story points out nicely the importance of persevering, as well as the importance of gaining the necessary knowledge to succeed.

The Horror, the Horror!

When you think of horror, one of the names that immediately springs to mind is Stephen King, the maestro of the chilling stories. Well, the world would have been a much different place if not for his wife. When King was writing his first novel, *Carrie*, he didn't like it, which is actually a problem with many writers.

However, he disliked his manuscript so much that he threw it out. He was just about done with writing. He'd had some success with his short stories, but it wasn't enough to pay the bills. He was already working as a teacher and working at a factory during the summer. He was ready to quit writing.

His wife Tabitha found the manuscript and rescued it. She encouraged him to submit it, and the rest is history. Think of all of the stories and movies that the world would have missed had he actually quit. We wouldn't have *The Shawshank Redemption*, *It*, *The Stand*, and *Stand by Me* (based on his short story "The Body"), for starters.

The Fab Five?

Do you know the name Stuart Sutcliffe? If you do, you are a massive fan of a little band called The Beatles. If not, chances are you still know The Beatles. Everyone knows them, but few know Sutcliffe. He was the original bassist for the band, and helped Lennon name the band. However, in 1961, he decided that he would enroll in the Hamburg College of Art rather than pursue music as a career. After all, what were the chances that the band would take off? Of course, we all know the story of the band and their spectacular rise to fame.

The Moral of These Stories...

It's simple. Don't quit. Do what you love and follow your passion. As obstacles are encountered, be creative to overcome them.

"Most great people have attained their greatest success just one step beyond their greatest failure."

— Napoleon Hill, Author Think and Grow Rich

Chapter 7:
How Do You Make Decisions & Solve Problems?

You WILL run into challenges and problems – probably every day. Not just from starting a new business but in many areas of your life. What is a problem? It is the difference between where you are and what you have, and where you want to be and what you want to have.

We have already discussed some of the problems you might face and possible ways to solve them. Starting with do you really want to be a Silver Entrepreneur, what business to start, how to get funding, how to stay motivated and now the million other small and large problems you will face and how to be a more creative problem solver.

There is so much more that could be included in the above chapters but it doesn't compare with the amount of valuable information, technologies, systems and new research that is available in this area. This chapter will provide an overview of topics that will help you be more creative, innovative and a better Silver Entrepreneur.

Good News for Silver Entrepreneurs

This is an area where you may have an advantage over younger entrepreneurs. You have a lot more experiences that give you more information to draw on and combine for new solutions. Most new ideas are a combination of already known products or concepts that we put together to make something new. Memories that have been buried for years frequently resurface just when you need them.

The other good news is that as we age, our brains continue to have the capacity to grow. Forty years ago we were told that our brain has a finite number of brain cells or neurons that continue to die as we age, but we now know that is not true and that we continue to make new connections throughout our lives unless the brain is damaged from accidents or disease.

How to Enhance Creative and Innovative Thinking

Creative thinking is the ability to come up with new or unique ideas, patterns or relationships. There are two types of creative thinking. The first is *analytic,* where the new idea or concept comes from combining two or more known concepts making something new. For example combining a phone and a camera and a computer to make a smart phone. Analytic creativity can come from deliberate searching using techniques for coming up with new ideas.

The other type of creative thinking, called *insight*, is where a new idea comes into our mind from out of the blue. It can be a totally new concept that is totally unique to us, such as the first thoughts of making an airplane before there were airplanes. The techniques to enhance our analytic and insight creativity can be quite different and will be explored in more detail in future books.

Although frequently used interchangeably with creative, the word innovative means more than just having new ideas. We all have some degree of creative ideas all the time. Many of our ideas are not new to the world but new to us. Innovations are when a creative idea is acted on and taken to an industry where it has not previously been introduced. This is where an entrepreneur has an opportunity to create a new business venture.

New research in brain and behavioral science has uncovered ways to expand our cognitive capabilities at any age. Some of the tried-and-true as well as the new-and-true ways to think more creatively include:

- Believe in your ability to find new ideas. If you don't expect to find an idea you won't put any effort into it. The more confidence you have about coming up with a good idea, the more persistent you will be.
- A positive attitude is important in starting or growing any business. It not only keeps you motivated, but it has been found that positive people are more creative. There is a time to switch to critical thinking when evaluating and judging the merit of a new ideas.

- Become more curious in a variety of subjects. The more diverse our storehouse of concepts and information the more combinations we can put together to make a new idea.
- Networking is important because successful businesses are not created alone. Test your ideas and uncover new ideas through discussions with others. Brain storm, join a master mind group or recruit partners to help resolve problems.

- There is old and new research on how our environment contributes to our creativity. More insight ideas are encouraged in a relaxed or meditative space rather than a rushed or tense atmosphere. Open spaces such as outdoors also encourage our insightful brains more than a closed or confined room.

• As previously mentioned, our brains, like the rest of our body, work best with good nutrition, exercise and the right amount of sleep.

Problem Solving System

As previously mentioned, a problem can be defined as anything that you want to have or know that you presently don't have or know. The key to becoming a good problem solver is following some specific steps and developing a skill for being creative. Some of the simplest ways to support your brain health to become more creative were given in the paragraphs above. The following section provides the seven steps that will improve your ability to solve problems.

Step One: Define the Problem

"It can be harder to define the problem than find the solution."

- Charles Darwin

Defining the problem is the most important part of problem solving. If we don't get it right all other steps could be a waste of time. How a problem is defined determines the possible solutions. For example: by saying "I need to write and publish a book for my expert program that teaches my ideas and experience" would lead you to creating an outline, writing a book, making multiple edits, creating a cover, writing a promotional description, getting a publisher or self publishing, getting the book to distributors, promoting, etc. But if you said "I need to have a book written and published for my expert program," that would open the possibility of writing an outline and having a ghostwriter, illustrator, or editor write a book (like many best sellers) then going to Amazon to have it published, distributed and promoted. By changing the wording of the problem it may solve the problem faster, easier, and possibly at a lower cost.

Most problems are part of a group or hierarchy of problems; solving the wrong problem may not help the real problem. For example, you may decide that to get more sales you need a better marketing plan when you actually need to add a product feature that most customers want. Or you may decide the product needs to be improved when all you really need is to have more people know the product is available and they would buy.

One of the toughest things in defining a problem is making sure it is not defined too broad or too narrow. Simple examples are: if your product is only for accountants you don't need to have a way for households to get your marketing information, or if it is a product for home finance you need to target more than accountants.

Thinking about a problem in isolation is also a problem with problem solving. Think about all the ramifications solving a problem will have on other parts of business or people. Solving one problem frequently opens or creates another problem. For example, if you decide assembling your product is too difficult for customers and decide to preassemble it, will it be so large that the packaging and shipping costs will make it prohibitively expensive?

Sometimes the problem may be able to be split into multiple or sub-problems making them easier to solve separately.

Ask the following questions to help find define your problem:

- What is the higher level problem? Lower level?
- Is this a cause or an effect?
- Why is it a problem?
- Why are we doing it?

- What purpose does it serve?

Sometimes finding a root cause of problem can be the solution in itself.

Step Two: Gather All the Information Available

"If I had an hour to solve a problem I'd spend 55 minutes thinking about the problem and 5 minutes thinking about solutions."

\- Albert Einstein

The second step in problem solving is gathering all the information you can that is associated with the problem. The more you know about all aspects around the issue, the better chance of finding a creative solution.

You may already know a lot about the industry from past experience and still benefit from doing research. You may not see the forest for the trees. Usually disruptive ideas come from a little outside the industry where they can see from a broader perspective.

Market research: Primary & Secondary research:

- Primary: do it yourself; surveys, interviews, trade shows to talk to and meet associated industry people.

- Secondary: Learn industry trends: from trade magazines, government reports, censes, trade associations, Google search (Google Trends by industry info on trends, sales, & demographics); SBDC (Small Business Development Corporation); Facebook

Categorize the type of problem and then look for places with similar problems that found solutions. Start with competitors, other industries, other sciences or entertainment.

Be observant as you ask yourself these questions:

- What do I know, need to know?
- What is important & unimportant?
- What is the history and future?
- Associated topics & issues?
- Who is involved, competition?
- What are the deeper purposes, meaning?
- Reasons for and against?
- Other ways or philosophies?
- What are the patterns or changes in patterns?

Once you have a greater understanding of all aspects of the problem, if you haven't already discovered the solution, it is time to develop ideas.

Step Three: Search for Ideas

"Hiding your sources is the key to creativity."

— Einstein

"Good artists copy, great artists steal."

— Picasso

Coming up with creative ideas can come from breaking an issue down into its elements and recombining with other known elements — the less obvious the recombination, the more creative it is.

In the book *Borrowing Brilliance* by David Kord Murray, he explains how new ideas are borrowed from other familiar elements possibly from within your industry or from outside your industry. This is true of nearly every new idea, design, methodology, or business. If it is combining a camera, phone, GPS, and computer it is considered genius. If it is a simple modification of a competitors product it may be considered copying, stealing, or plagiarism.

When a conscious process is used to break down aspects of an item and recombine with other elements, psychologists call it "analytic" thought. When this kind of creative recombination takes place in an instant, it's called an insight.

Using metaphors may help you see how the problem compares to other problems. Metaphors and analogy are the way we think, we compare new things to what we already know, we use metaphors subconsciously and can become better problem solvers when we can use them consciously.

When you run out of ideas these techniques can trigger thinking from new directions. The following list includes some of the ways elements can be manipulated to make new ideas.

- Combining – a toothbrush with a motor for an electric toothbrush
- Rearrangement – moving the elements in time to make a movie that starts at the end of an event and works back to the beginning
- Substitution – replacing plastic for glass in bottles making them cheaper, safer and lighter weight
- Association – using "A Dummies Guide" in a book title makes an association of a simple easy method to learn
- Adaptation – using an unmanned drone to deliver packages from Amazon
- Magnification – using projection technology to magnify the smaller image of the conventional TV

- Minimization – breeding dogs to smaller sizes opened a market for many miniature breeds
- Adding & Subtracting – adding a mouse to the computer revolutionized the industry and removing the mouse in place of touch pads and touch screens, did it again

Step Four: Forget About It

It is a common experience that a problem difficult at night is resolved in the morning after the committee of sleep has worked on it.

— John Steinbeck

The 4th step is letting a problem incubate in the subconscious. After a significant amount of time has been spent working on a problem, it can be more productive to walk away from it and stop thinking about it. It will still be in the subconscious mind and the subconscious can be better at making combinations because it works with parallel ideas, unlike the conscious mind which uses serial thinking.

We have all had ideas come to us when we are in a sleep state, just before or after waking, or relaxing in a shower. We can also create that conducive mental state through meditation.

When you are letting a problem incubate it can also be useful to let the mind think about other problems. Because then you are using the same part of the brain that is used for creative thought; as opposed to watching TV or idle chat.

If you're letting a problem incubate for an extended period of time, you'll want to come back to the problem daily to at least review and possibly add a few ideas for solutions.

Step Five: Critical Judging

"If your only tool is a hammer then every problem looks like a nail."

– Abraham Maslow

The 5th step is critical thinking. Up to now, you want to keep an open mind and not eliminate ideas too quickly because some of the best solutions frequently seem impractical until they are developed further. But at this stage it is necessary for innovation – recognizing the challenges and making judgments on what will and won't work is essential at the right time. All positive thinking can lead to bad ideas and wasted time, so:

- Identify the strength and weaknesses of your idea

- Use positive and negative judgment
- Left and right brain for logical and intuitive analysis

Make a list of the positives and negatives for the ideas you came up with, then think about where you can go to find solutions to the negative issues that still need to be resolved.

Go to right brain thinking to see if you're intuitive mind (gut feel, subconscious) feels if it is right. If it doesn't feel right, continue to analyze why it may not be a good or the best idea. This type of intuitive feeling has made a big difference in many important decisions. See the book "Blink" by Malcolm Gladwell for many examples.

Step Six: Complete or Repeat

"If you wait for perfect conditions, you will never get anything done."

— Ecclesiastes 11:4

Step 6 is complete or repeat. If you don't feel you have a good solution yet (or want to find another or better one) go back through steps 1-5. There are always more and better solutions but beware of being a perfectionist.

Although I have numbered the steps in a logical process for problem solving, the creative process is not linear nor circular; it is a combination. It is useful to learn the steps and follow them for some types of projects but the process is different for different problems, different circumstances and for different people or teams.

It is always a good idea to relook at the problem, rethink the question, or analyze if you are going in the right direction. Getting lost in the details can cause you to go off track and miss the big picture. Some people can be focused on the details and stay conscious of the big picture, but most of us need to step back and relook at the problem we are solving and our assumptions; in other words to see the forest from the trees. For example, while some authors can write a book in one sitting, keeping the theme and ending with all the sentence structure and grammar correct and ready to print without needing any edits, most of us would need many edits and rewrites to get it right. Both methods can create great products.

Step Seven: Take Action Immediately

"The secret of getting ahead is getting started."

\- Mark Twain

"You'll discover once underway, that you know more than you know you know."

- Price Pritchett

Step seven is when you think you have the right idea take action. Depending on the type of problem, idea or project you are working on you probably want to break this step into a couple parts. The first action you would usually want to take is to test your solution or idea.

Testing can save you significant time and expense. Do an experiment to determine the feasibility, market potential, manufacturability, or just to evaluate if it has the appeal you expected. The test may be building a prototype, running an idea by a sample of customers, or completing a segment of a design or methodology.

If your idea is going to fail, the sooner the better. Failure at an early stage, before major investment of time or money may be considered a blessing rather than a failure. You may want to begin testing before you think you are ready. If the idea seems to be a possible solution – test it.

Many very successful people and businesses have the philosophy of fail fast, fail often and fail forward. Almost every company has had failures before success. Thomas J. Watson, the CEO of IBM once said "Would you like me to give you a formula for success? It's quite simple, really. Double your rate of failure".

As a silver entrepreneur you have probably learned this lesson many times. We have all made wrong decisions and failed but have survived and frequently been better because of it. What is important is to take any type of action and do something, because action starts the momentum that could lead to great success. Bad action may be better than no action, remember you can fail your way to success.

An idea that is not used is as good as no idea at all.

The way to get started is to quit talking and start doing.

– Walt Disney

Conclusion

Now that you've come to the end of the book, you should be a bit better prepared to start your new business no matter what it might be. You've learned ways to come up with a business idea, to finance the business, and even some marketing tips. Most importantly, you understand the importance of starting, sticking with it, and not quitting.

Silver entrepreneurs just like you are already out there doing it. They are achieving success, and you can do the same. All you need to do is to be willing to take those first steps and to keep learning. This book on the basics of getting started is your first step. So, let's go and make history.

Whatever the mind can conceive and believe,
the mind can achieve.

– Napoleon Hill

About The Author

Joe started more than a dozen business ventures and, while they were not all successful, each provided valuable learning experiences. Several new ventures were started after the age of 60 with more expected. An engineering education provided the starting point for science and technology jobs that developed into executive positions and businesses startups. Continuing curiosity and study into entrepreneurial business practices, personal development, and behavior sciences led to training, speaking, writing, and consulting for business startups and entrepreneurs.

To contact the author for additional information on other programs or consulting please Joe.Schneider@me.com

FREE GIFT

Thank you for purchasing this book. There is a FREE gift waiting for you by going to: https://realliving.leadpages.co/gift-v1/

When you go there you will find a valuable download to support your success as a Silver Entrepreneur. At times the free gift will change so you may want to check back from time-to-time.

www.ingramcontent.com/pod-product-compliance
Lightning Source LLC
Chambersburg PA
CBHW060420190526
45169CB00002B/985